PATEK PHILIPPE®
HIGHLIGHTS

HERBERT JAMES

4880 Lower Valley Road • Atglen, PA 19310

Other Schiffer Books by the author:
Omega Highlights. ISBN: 978-0-7643-4212-7. $29.99
A. Lange & Söhne Highlights.
    ISBN: 978-0-7643-4361-2. $29.99
Breitling Highlights. ISBN: 978-0-7643-4211-0. $29.99

Other Schiffer Books on Related Subjects:
Breitling: The History of a Great Brand of Watches 1884 to the
    Present. Benno Richter. ISBN: 9780764326707. $49.95
Omega Designs: Feast for the Eyes. Anton Kreuzer.
    ISBN: 9780764329951. $59.99
Rolex Wristwatches: An Unauthorized History. James M.
    Dowling & Jeffrey P. Hess. ISBN: 0764324373. $125.00
Swiss Wristwatches: Chronology of Worldwide Success.
    Gisbert L. Brunner & Christian Pfeiffer-Belli.
    ISBN: 0887403018. $69.95
Vintage Rolex® Sports Models - 3rd Edition.
    Martin Skeet & Nick Urul. ISBN: 9780764329814. $79.99
Wristwatch Chronometers. Fritz von Osterhausen.
    ISBN: 0764303759. $79.95

Originally published as *Patek Philippe Highlights*
© 2010 HEEL Verlag GmbH
Editor: Herbert James
English Translation: Elizabeth Doerr
Design and Layout: Muser Medien GmbH,
Mannheim Tanja Küppershaus

English Version Copyright © 2013
by Schiffer Publishing, Ltd.

Library of Congress Control Number: 2013943324

"Schiffer," "Schiffer Publishing, Ltd. & Design," and the "Design of pen and inkwell" are registered trademarks of Schiffer Publishing, Ltd.

Cover by Justin Watkinson
Type set in Tall Films Expanded /Avant Garde Gothic Itc

ISBN: 978-0-7643-4322-3
Printed in China

Published by Schiffer Publishing, Ltd.
4880 Lower Valley Road
Atglen, PA 19310
Phone: (610) 593-1777; Fax: (610) 593-2002
E-mail: Info@schifferbooks.com

For our complete selection of fine books on this and related subjects, please visit our website at www.schifferbooks.com. You may also write for a free catalog.

This book may be purchased from the publisher. Please try your bookstore first.

We are always looking for people to write books on new and related subjects. If you have an idea for a book, please contact us at proposals@schifferbooks.com.

Schiffer Publishing's titles are available at special discounts for bulk purchases for sales promotions or premiums. Special editions, including personalized covers, corporate imprints, and excerpts can be created in large quantities for special needs. For more information, contact the publisher.

CONTENTS

1.................... **Brand History**................... Page 6

2.................... **Historical Models**.......... Page 16
A selection of Patek Philippe's most well known
wristwatch models

3.................... **Complications** .... Page 30
From chronographs through world time watches
all the way to the annual calendar

4.................... **Grand Complications**...... Page 44
Highly complicated and fascinating: the best that
watchmaking has to offer

5.................... **Calatrava**.................. Page 60
The grand classics of Patek Philippe's collection

6.................... **Nautilus** .... Page 72
Patek Philippe in sports dress: the Nautilus was
introduced in 1976

7.................... **Aquanaut** .... Page 80
The "little brother" of the Nautilus model is a watch
for every aspect of life

8.................... **Ellipse d'Or** .... Page 86
Unmistakable: ideal proportions characterize this
model

9.................... **Gondolo** .... Page 90
The design language of the 1930s freshly
interpreted

PATEK PHILIPPE
PREFACE

Patek Philippe is a prestigious name in the watch industry; it possesses a status that really no other brand can boast. In more than 160 years, the venerable Swiss manufacture has become a synonym for highly complicated watches of the most noble quality.

Alongside an extensive look at the history of Patek Philippe, this book presents you with more than 100 of the most beautiful and sought-after models the exclusive Genevan brand has manufactured. From the legendary models of the 1930s through the diversification of the post-war decades retaining the brand's inimitable design language to the current top models approaching grand complication status, Patek Philippe's products have always been impressive. The following pages will help you form an overview of what has helped create the brand's global reputation, propelling it to the peak of horology's Olympus: the art of mechanical watchmaking incorporating the highest degree of complexity, innovation, and pioneering design. Almost without competition.

The selection and details presented in this book can only be a representative cross section of the innumerable models and variations Patek Philippe has created throughout the years. We'd like to take you on this journey of browsing, looking, and dreaming. Certainly you will find one treasure or another in the following pages to capture your interest and inspire you to take a closer look–either in your neighborhood retailer's cases or in more in-depth horological literature. Enjoy!

Herbert James

BRAND HISTORY

The origins of today's horological king, Patek Philippe, are inseparable from the city of Geneva even though they are actually to be found rather far from the modern seat of watchmaking: in Poland. Nonetheless, this name has stood for the greatest degree of perfection that *haute horlogerie* has to offer.

The young officer Antoni Norbert Patek de Prawdzic took part in an uprising that opposed the hated Russian occupation in 1830–the year in which half of Europe was once again in flames thanks to the July revolution beginning in France after it had enjoyed one and a half decades of relative peace. The uprising Patek de Prawdzic took part in had the independence of Poland as its goal. The czar's troops were at first run out, but they came back in 1831 and finally conquered Warsaw in September of 1832. Patek de Prawdzic, along with about 50,000 other rebels, fled to the area occupied by the German empire before moving on to France, where he set type for a living. From there he continued on to Geneva.

ONE OF THE WORLD'S
COSTLIEST WATCHES IS MADE
OF STEEL

Like the great swords of
another age, Nautilus took shape
between the skilled hands
of master craftsmen. Like sword
and knight, Nautilus and its owner
are meant to be inseparable for life.
Nautilus, with its hand-finished

Patek Philippe self-winding
movement, will accompany
you when you dive.
Or when the occasion
is formal or festive. Or when
you set out to slay dragons
in the boardroom.

PATEK PHILIPPE
GENÈVE

Catalogue and list of nearest jeweler from Dept. NG. Patek Philippe S.A.,
41 rue du Rhône, 1211 Geneva 3, Switzerland

Nickel-chrome-molyb-
denum steel case is water-
resistant to depth of 120
meters (396 feet). The swinging
mass which winds the watch while
you wear it incorporates a piece
of solid 21 kt. gold (added
weight ensures optimum winding
efficiency). Amazingly slim case
with matching steel bracelet.

The city of Geneva also had a few temperamental decades behind it by this time: after the bourgeoisie and working classes established a democratic constitution, in 1781, its demise just one year later forced many early industrialists and upper class members into emigration. Under Napoleon the city was integrated into the French state and became known as the Département du Léman. After the fall of the self-crowned emperor, the city-state Geneva was founded and folded into the newly founded Swiss canton of Geneva just one year later. The ensuing years saw Geneva experience an economic upswing, which could, above all, be attributed to the creation of the craftsmen's and artisans' manufactures. The Europe of the Restoration era needed luxury items, whether it was to underscore aristocratic claim to power or to illustrate the success of manufacture owners and the first large industrialists.

Patek de Prawdzic settled in the surrounding area of the enamellers, goldsmiths, engravers, and—of course—watchmakers and was at first employed as a reassembler. He established a supply network of high-quality watch movements and had them encased in his own workshops, a principle that many watch brands practice to this day. Patek de Prawdzic was so successful with this work that he could hardly meet the demand for his watches. For this reason, he looked for a partner in order to increase the size of his company. He therefore founded the company Patek, Czapek & Co in 1839 with Franciszek Czapek, a watchmaker also of Polish extraction. A building on the right bank of the Rhône was chosen as the company headquarters, across from the present headquarters.

In the first five years, the young company produced about 200 pocket watches per year with the aid of half a dozen employees. In 1841, the company founder became a citizen of Geneva—and thus a Swiss citizen—from which point on he called himself Antoine Norbert de Patek.

De Patek traveled to Paris with his products in 1844 in order to present them to a wider audience. It was there that he met the young Parisian watchmaker Jean-Adrien Philippe, who was said to have developed an innovative winding mechanism: his pocket watches disposed of a crown winding mechanism, which required a key. Thus it became possible to visibly reduce the height of the pocket watch, for it no longer had any use for the clumsy square element needed to wind the mainspring and set the time, using the laborious motion of the key. The public hardly took notice of this invention, but de Patek immediately recognized the potential of the innovation, which could well revolutionize watchmaking.

Since the relationship between business partners de Patek and Czapek had already started to sour over the last few years, de Patek used the occasion to ask thirty-year-old Philippe to become the new partner of his company in Geneva. The Parisian watchmaker agreed and became co-owner after Czapek's contract ended on May 15, 1845. Patek & Co., owned by Jean-Adrien Philippe, Antoine Norbert de Patek, and the young lawyer Vincent Gostkowski, moved into its new premises just a few houses down from the old one on Quai des Bergues 15.

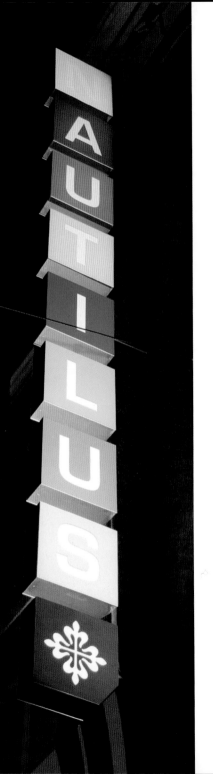

The cooperation of the two men proved, in the following years, to be a windfall for the company. Though Philippe at first continued working in Paris, he finally gave up his shop there and moved to Geneva in order to transform the workshop from its purely manual method of production into a more industrial style of manufacture, using division of labor. Thanks to the inventions and innovations of the young French watchmaker, what became Patek Philippe & Co. on January 1, 1851, also took on a leading position in the area of development and utilization of mechanical tools.

De Patek ensured that the company became well known in Europe and America, winning clients there. During business trips that would often stretch for months at a time, he made a great deal of contacts and sold a great number of watches. This ensured a consistent influx of funds, a condition that secured the opportunities to extend production facilities and improve them.

Philippe continued with his horological innovations. In 1868, the manufacture completed their first wristwatch, for Polish Countess Kocewicz—probably the first wristwatch in the history of Swiss watchmaking. In 1889 he designed the first watch movement to contain a "perpetual" date, the display of which needed no correction despite differing lengths of months and even leap years. The perpetual calendars found in Patek Philippe's modern collection are based on this exceptional horological achievement.

In 1877 de Patek passed away. Philippe continued to lead the company until his death in 1894. After his passing, the employees of the company acquired partnership. Philippe's son-in-law, Joseph-Antoine Benassy-Philippe, took over the management of the company. Under his leadership it was transformed into a limited company in 1901 called Ancienne Manufacture d'Horlogerie Patek Philippe & Co. SA.

At the end of the 1920s, however, the successful manufacture faltered: the Great Depression that was caused by the stock market crash of Black Thursday on October 24, 1929, suddenly decimated the capital that financed the continuously in-demand luxury products. An offer of purchase by David LeCoultre, who had already been supplying Patek Philippe with ébauches since 1905, was rejected. Instead, brothers Charles and Jean Stern, who at the time were the dial makers for the Genevan brand, were able to buy the majority of the company in 1932. The last of the owners belonging to the founding families, Joseph Emile Philippe, grandson of Jean-Adrien Philippe, lost his stake during this move.

Under the aegis of the Stern brothers and their managing director Jean Pfister, the company once again established itself as an innovative manufacture by developing and manufacturing its own movements. At the same time, it advanced to become a style icon in the area of elegant men's watches with the models it introduced at the beginning of the 1930s. Above all it was the Calatrava, launched in 1932, that was responsible for this achievement, and which continues to uphold it in the modern era.

Philippe Stern and his son Thierry, who has led the company since 2009.

During this period in time, the finest wristwatches that the world had seen up to that point were being manufactured in Patek Philippe's workshops. Alongside the simple, timeless models, the company created, most notably, numerous horological complications, from the perpetual calendar to the tourbillon, often combined with chronographs. The creations emerging from this era founded the exclusive, almost mythical, reputation that the brand enjoys to this day. Watches from this epoch are therefore particularly in demand and have achieved the highest results at auctions for years. Patek Philippe continues to remain in the hands of the Stern family

and is thus not housed under the roof of a large corporation. Philippe Stern recently passed the scepter to his son Thierry, who plans to continue the consistently upward direction of the brand based on the achievements of the past, combined with innovative creations in terms of horological developments.

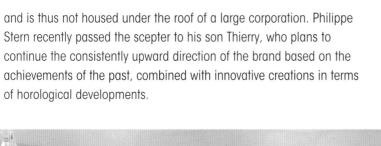

HISTORICAL MODELS

From 1932, Patek Philippe's workshops were manufacturing the finest wristwatches in the world. In addition to great complications, such as perpetual calendars, exquisite chronographs, and highly complex tourbillons, the brand laid the foundations for its almost mythical reputation during this era with its exceptionally simple, yet finely crafted men's watches. It is largely thanks to this epoch in the company history that the manufacture enjoys such a stately reputation today, and that the creations from the 1930s and '40s now attain the highest prices at auction that have ever been paid for wristwatches.

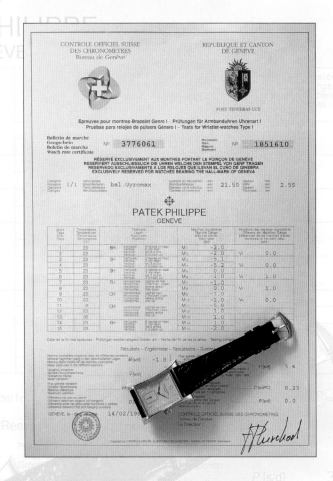

CHRONOGRAPH PERPETUAL CALENDAR (1942)

Reference: 1518

Movement: manual winding, rhodium-plated, côtes de Genève, column-wheel control of chronograph

Functions: hours, minutes, subsidiary seconds; chronograph; perpetual calendar with date, weekday, month, moon phase

Case: stainless steel, ø 35 mm; push-down case back

Remarks: only two of these models were ever manufactured in stainless steel; most expensive wristwatch ever auctioned in Germany

Estimated value: $1,800,000 (€ 1.400.000,–)
(2009)

CHRONOGRAPH PERPETUAL CALENDAR (1945)

Reference: 1518

Movement: manual winding, rhodium-plated, côtes de Genève, column-wheel control of chronograph

Functions: hours, minutes, subsidiary seconds; chronograph; perpetual calendar with date, weekday, month, moon phase

Case: yellow gold, ø 35 mm; push-down case back

Remarks: extremely rare chronograph from the series of only 281 ever made

Estimated value: $260,000 (€ 200.000,–)
(2009)

TECHNICAL DATA

PERPETUAL CALENDAR (1963)

Reference:	3448
Movement:	automatic, Patek Philippe Caliber 27-460Q, rhodium-plated, côtes de Genève, Seal of Geneva
Functions:	hours, minutes; perpetual calendar with date, weekday, month, moon phase
Case:	white gold, ø 37 mm; push-down case back
Remarks:	extremely rare men's watch; only 586 pieces were produced between 1962 and 1982
Estimated value: (2009)	$195,000 (€ 150.000,–)

PERPETUAL CALENDAR (1970)

Reference:	3448
Movement:	automatic, Patek Philippe Caliber 27-460Q, rhodium-plated, fausses côtes decoration, 18-karat gold rotor, Seal of Geneva
Functions:	hours, minutes; perpetual calendar with date, weekday, month, moon phase
Case:	yellow gold, ø 37 mm; push-down case back
Estimated value: (2009)	$104,000 (€ 80.000,–)

ONE-BUTTON CHRONOGRAPH (1936)

Reference:	130
Movement:	manual winding, Patek Philippe Caliber 13''', rhodium-plated, fausses côtes decoration, column-wheel control of chronograph
Functions:	hours, minutes, subsidiary seconds; chronograph
Case:	yellow gold, ø 33 mm; push-down case back
Remarks:	chronograph button integrated into crown
Estimated value: (2009)	$390,000 (€ 300.000,–)

CHRONOGRAPH (1938)

Movement:	manual winding, Patek Philippe Caliber 13'''-130, rhodium-plated, fausses côtes decoration, column-wheel control of chronograph
Functions:	hours, minutes, subsidiary seconds; chronograph
Case:	yellow gold, ø 33 mm; push-down case back
Estimated value: (2009)	$65,000 (€ 50.000,–)

TECHNICAL DATA

SPLIT-SECONDS CHRONOGRAPH (1939)

Reference:	1436
Movement:	manual winding, rhodium-plated, fausses côtes decoration, column-wheel control of chronograph, Seal of Geneva
Functions:	hours, minutes, subsidiary seconds; split-seconds chronograph
Case:	yellow gold, ø 33 mm; push-down case back
Remarks:	only 38 pieces were made of this extremely rare chronograph in yellow gold with a silver dial
Estimated value: (2009)	$220,000 (€ 170.000,–)

CHRONOGRAPH (1945)

Reference:	130
Movement:	manual winding, Patek Philippe Caliber 13, rhodium-plated, côtes de Genève, column-wheel control of chronograph
Functions:	hours, minutes, subsidiary seconds; chronograph
Case:	stainless steel, ø 34 mm; push-down case back
Estimated value: (2009)	$104,000 (€ 80.000,–)

MEN'S WATCH (1932)

Movement:	manual winding, frosted finish, gold-plated
Functions:	hours, minutes, subsidiary seconds
Case:	yellow gold, 26 x 44 mm; push-down case back
Estimated value: **(2009)**	$23,000 (€ 18.000,–)

MEN'S WATCH (1936)

Reference:	417
Movement:	manual winding, Patek Philippe Caliber 9-90, rhodium-plated, fausses côtes decoration
Functions:	hours, minutes, subsidiary seconds
Case:	platinum, 20 x 36 mm; push-down case back
Remarks:	engraving "S.S. Magoffin" on case back
Estimated value: **(2009)**	$25,000 (€ 19.000,–)

MEN'S WATCH (1937)

Reference:	520
Movement:	manual winding, Patek Philippe Caliber 9-90, rhodium-plated, fausses côtes decoration
Functions:	hours, minutes, subsidiary seconds
Case:	yellow gold, 24 x 40 mm; push-down case back
Estimated value: **(2009)**	$14,200 (€ 11.000,–)

MEN'S WATCH (1938)

Reference:	520
Movement:	Patek Philippe Caliber 9-90, rhodium-plated, fausses côtes decoration, high-polished screws, shaped movement
Functions:	hours, minutes, subsidiary seconds
Case:	yellow gold, 24 x 40 mm; push-down case back
Estimated value: **(2009)**	$14,200 (€ 11.000,–)

CALATRAVA (1938)

Movement:	manual winding, Patek Philippe Caliber 12-120, rhodium-plated, côtes de Genève
Functions:	hours, minutes, subsidiary seconds
Case:	yellow gold, ø 36 mm; push-down case back
Estimated value: (2009)	$9,000 (€ 7000,–)

CALATRAVA (1949)

Reference:	565
Movement:	manual winding, Patek Philippe Caliber 12‴-120, rhodium-plated, fausses côtes decoration
Functions:	hours, minutes, subsidiary seconds
Case:	stainless steel, ø 35 mm; screw-down case back, additional movement protection cap
Estimated value: (2009)	$19,400 (€ 15.000,–)

CALATRAVA (1953)

Reference:	2509
Movement:	manual winding, Patek Philippe Caliber 12-400, rhodium-plated, côtes de Genève, Seal of Geneva
Functions:	hours, minutes, subsidiary seconds
Case:	yellow gold, ø 35 mm; screw-down case back
Estimated value: (2009)	$19,400 (€ 15.000,–)

CALATRAVA (1960)

Reference:	2509
Movement:	Patek Philippe Caliber 12'''-400, rhodium-plated, fausses côtes decoration, Seal of Geneva
Functions:	hours, minutes, subsidiary seconds
Case:	stainless steel, ø 35 mm; screw-down case back, additional movement protection cap
Estimated value: (2009)	$45,000 (€ 35.000,–)

MEN'S AUTOMATIC WATCH (1956)

Reference:	2551
Movement:	automatic, Patek Philippe Caliber 12-600AT, rhodium-plated, côtes de Genève, gold rotor
Functions:	hours, minutes, subsidiary seconds
Case:	yellow gold, ø 36 mm; screw-down case back
Estimated value: (2009)	$14,200 (€ 11.000,–)

MEN'S AUTOMATIC WATCH (1962)

Reference:	3445
Movement:	automatic, Patek Philippe Caliber 27-460M, rhodium-plated, côtes de Genève, gold rotor, Seal of Geneva
Functions:	hours, minutes, subsidiary seconds; date
Case:	yellow gold, ø 35 mm; screw-down case back
Estimated value: (2009)	$10,300 (€ 8000,–)

MEN'S AUTOMATIC WATCH (1954)

Reference:	2526
Movement:	automatic, Patek Philippe Caliber 12-600 AT, rhodium-plated, côtes de Genève, gold rotor, Seal of Geneva
Functions:	hours, minutes, subsidiary seconds
Case:	platinum, ø 35 mm; screw-down case back
Remarks:	diamond-set dial
Estimated value: (2009)	$77,400 (€ 60.000,–)

MEN'S AUTOMATIC WATCH (1971)

Reference:	2526
Movement:	automatic, Patek Philippe Caliber 12-600 AT, rhodium-plated, côtes de Genève, gold rotor, Seal of Geneva
Functions:	hours, minutes, subsidiary seconds
Case:	red gold, ø 35 mm; screw-down case back
Remarks:	enamel dial
Estimated value: (2009)	$51,600 (€ 40.000,–)

MEN'S AUTOMATIC WATCH (1963)

Reference: 3429
Movement: automatic, Patek Philippe Caliber 27-460, rhodium-plated, gold rotor
Functions: hours, minutes, subsidiary seconds
Case: white gold, ø 35 mm; screw-down case back
Estimated value: $18,100 (€ 14.000,–)
(2009)

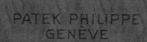

MEN'S AUTOMATIC WATCH (1971)

Reference:	3445
Movement:	automatic, Patek Philippe Caliber 27-460/PM, rhodium-plated, gold rotor, Seal of Geneva
Functions:	hours, minutes, subsidiary seconds; date
Case:	white gold, ø 35 mm; screw-down case back
Estimated value: (2009)	$19,400 (€ 15.000,–)

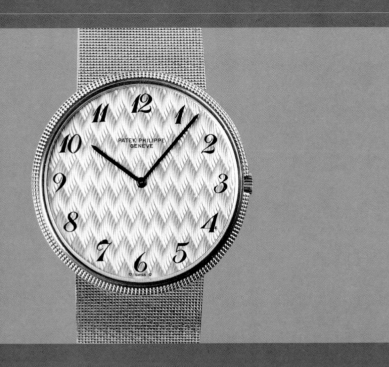

MEN'S AUTOMATIC WATCH (1972)

Reference:	3588/1
Movement:	automatic, Patek Philippe Caliber 28-255, rhodium-plated, fausses côtes decoration, gold rotor, Seal of Geneva
Functions:	hours, minutes
Case:	white gold, ø 35 mm; screw-down case back
Estimated value: (2009)	$8,400 (€ 6.500,–)

MEN'S AUTOMATIC WATCH (1982)

Reference:	3569-3
Movement:	automatic, Patek Philippe Caliber 1-350, rhodium-plated, côtes de Genève, gold rotor, Seal of Geneva
Functions:	hours, minutes
Case:	white gold, ø 35 mm; screw-down case back
Estimated value: (2009)	$6,500 (€ 5.000,–)

PATEK PHILIPPE
COMPLICATIONS

Normally a watch displays the time: hours, minutes, seconds. If a mechanical wristwatch is meant to show further information, in conjunction with the time and date, it becomes "complicated." Thus, the watches that have other practical functions, in addition to the basic ones, are called "complications." Patek Philippe offers a great number of "everyday" complications: the annual calendar so characteristic of this brand, various time zone and world time watches for modern globetrotters, moon phase displays, and of course chronographs for to-the-second timing of events. If several of these displays are combined within one watch, the gap between it and a so-called grand complication is not wide.

ANNUAL CALENDAR

Reference:	5205G
Movement:	automatic, Patek Philippe Caliber 324 S QA LU 24h
Functions:	hours, minutes, sweep seconds; annual calendar with date, weekday, month, moon phase; 24-hour display
Case:	white gold, ø 40 mm; sapphire crystal; transparent case back; water-resistant to 3 bar (30 m)
Price (2010):	$ 35,000 (€ 27.110,–)

ANNUAL CALENDAR

Reference:	5396G
Movement:	automatic, Patek Philippe Caliber 324 S QA LU 24h
Functions:	hours, minutes, sweep seconds;
	annual calendar with date, weekday, month, moon phase
Case:	white gold, ø 38 mm; sapphire crystal;
	transparent case back; water-resistant to 3 bar (30 m)
Price (2010):	$35,000 (€ 27.470,–)

ANNUAL CALENDAR

Reference:	5396G
Movement:	automatic, Patek Philippe Caliber 324 S QA LU 24h
Functions:	hours, minutes, sweep seconds;
	annual calendar with date, weekday, month, moon phase
Case:	white gold, ø 38 mm; sapphire crystal;
	transparent case back; water-resistant to 3 bar (30 m)
Price (2010):	$35,000 (€ 27.470,–)

ANNUAL CALENDAR

Reference:	5396G
Movement:	automatic,
	Patek Philippe Caliber 324 S QA LU 24h
Functions:	hours, minutes, sweep seconds;
	annual calendar with date,
	weekday, month, moon phase
Case:	white gold, ø 38 mm; sapphire crystal;
	transparent case back;
	water-resistant to 3 bar (30 m)
Price (2010):	$35,000 (€ 27.470,–)

TECHNICAL DATA

ANNUAL CALENDAR

Reference:	5146G
Movement:	automatic, Patek Philippe Caliber 315 S IRM QA LU
Functions:	hours, minutes, sweep seconds;
	annual calendar with date, weekday,
	month, moon phase; power reserve display
Case:	white gold, ø 39 mm; sapphire crystal;
	transparent case back; water-resistant to 3 bar (30 m)
Price (2010):	$30,660 (€ 23.760,–)

ANNUAL CALENDAR

Reference:	5146R
Movement:	automatic, Patek Philippe Caliber 315 S IRM QA LU
Functions:	hours, minutes, sweep seconds;
	annual calendar with date, weekday,
	month, moon phase; power reserve display
Case:	rose gold, ø 39 mm; sapphire crystal;
	transparent case back; water-resistant to 3 bar (30 m)
Price (2010):	$30,660 (€ 23.760,–)

ANNUAL CALENDAR

Reference:	5135G
Movement:	automatic, Patek Philippe Caliber 324 S QA LU 24h; Seal of Geneva
Functions:	hours, minutes, sweep seconds; annual calendar with date, weekday, month, moon phase: 24-hour display
Case:	white gold, 51 x 40.3 mm; sapphire crystal
Price (2008):	$33,600 (€ 26.000,–)

ANNUAL CALENDAR

Reference:	4936R
Movement:	automatic, Patek Philippe Caliber 315 S QA LU
Functions:	hours, minutes, sweep seconds;
	annual calendar with date, weekday, month, moon phase
Case:	rose gold, ø 37 mm; bezel set with 156 diamonds;
	sapphire crystal; transparent case back;
	water-resistant to 3 bar (30 m)
Remarks:	mother-of-pearl dial
Price (2010):	$34,160 (€ 26.470,–)

ANNUAL CALENDAR

Reference:	4936R
Movement:	automatic, Patek Philippe Caliber 315 S QA LU
Functions:	hours, minutes, sweep seconds;
	annual calendar with date, weekday, month, moon phase
Case:	yellow gold, ø 37 mm; bezel set with 156 diamonds;
	sapphire crystal; transparent case back;
	water-resistant to 3 bar (30 m)
Remarks:	mother-of-pearl dial
Price (2010):	$34,160 (€ 26.470,–)

ANNUAL CALENDAR

Reference: 4937G

Movement: automatic, Patek Philippe Caliber 324 S QA LU

Functions: hours, minutes, sweep seconds; annual calendar with date, weekday, month, moon phase

Case: white gold, ø 37 mm; bezel and strap lugs set with a total of 431 diamonds; crown set with 14 diamonds; sapphire crystal; transparent case back; water-resistant to 3 bar (30 m)

Price (2010): $51,660 (€ 40.030,–)

CHRONOGRAPH

Reference: 5170J

Movement: manual winding, Patek Philippe Caliber CH 29-535 PS; column-wheel control of chronograph

Functions: hours, minutes, subsidiary seconds; chronograph

Case: yellow gold, ø 39 mm; sapphire crystal; transparent case back; water-resistant to 3 bar (30 m)

Price (2010): $59,850 (€ 46.380,–)

CHRONOGRAPH

Reference:	5070
Movement:	manual winding, Patek Philippe Caliber CH 27-70
Functions:	hours, minutes, subsidiary seconds; chronograph
Case:	yellow gold, ø 42 mm; sapphire crystal; transparent case back; water-resistant to 3 bar (30 m)
Price (2009):	on request

ANNUAL CALENDAR CHRONOGRAPH

Reference:	5960R
Movement:	automatic, Patek Philippe Caliber CH 28-520 IRM QA 24H; column-wheel control of chronograph
Functions:	hours, minutes, sweep seconds; chronograph; annual calendar with date, weekday, month; power reserve display
Case:	rose gold, ø 40.5 mm; sapphire crystal; transparent case back
Price (2010):	$55,250 (€ 42.810,–)

ANNUAL CALENDAR CHRONOGRAPH

Reference:	5960P
Movement:	automatic, Patek Philippe Caliber CH 28-520 IRM QA 24H; column wheel control of chronograph
Functions:	hours, minutes, sweep seconds; chronograph; annual calendar with date, weekday, month; power reserve display
Case:	platinum, ø 40.5 mm; sapphire crystal; transparent case back
Price (2009):	$66,290 (€ 51.370,–)

ANNUAL CALENDAR CHRONOGRAPH

Reference:	5960P
Movement:	automatic, Patek Philippe Caliber CH 28-520 IRM QA 24H; column wheel control of chronograph
Functions:	hours, minutes, sweep seconds; chronograph; annual calendar with date, weekday, month; power reserve display
Case:	platinum, ø 40.5 mm; sapphire crystal; transparent case back
Price (2010):	$66,290 (€ 51.370,–)

WORLD TIME WATCH

Reference:	5131G
Movement:	automatic, Patek Philippe Caliber 240 HU
Functions:	hours, minutes; world time
Case:	white gold, ø 39.5 mm;
	dial disk with 24-hour display and world cities;
	sapphire crystal; transparent case back
Remarks:	enamel dial
Price (2010):	$46,960 (€ 36.390,–)

WORLD TIME WATCH

Reference:	5130P
Movement:	automatic, Patek Philippe Caliber 240 HU
Functions:	hours, minutes; world time
Case:	platinum, ø 39.5 mm;
	dial disk with 24-hour display and world cities;
	sapphire crystal; transparent case back
Price (2008):	$45,580 (€ 35.320,–)

WORLD TIME WATCH

Reference:	5130G
Movement:	automatic, Patek Philippe Caliber 240 HU
Functions:	hours, minutes; world time
Case:	white gold, ø 39.5 mm;
	dial disk with 24-hour display and world cities;
	sapphire crystal; transparent case back
Remarks:	enamel dial
Price (2007):	$28,520 (€ 22.100,–)

PATEK PHILIPPE
GRAND COMPLICATIONS

The grand complications are generally regarded as the crowning
glory of the art of watchmaking and unite incredible know-how with
great knowledge and decades of watchmaking experience. Only very
few watch brands in the world are in a position to enter this area of
haute horlogerie, and Patek Philippe has, since its founding in 1839,
been counted among them. No other manufacture can boast having
developed and produced so many timepieces of this highest degree,
whether split-seconds chronographs, perpetual calendars, tourbillons,
or repeaters—or any combination of these in one movement.

GRAND COMPLICATION REF. 5207

Reference:	5207
Movement:	manual winding, Patek Philippe Caliber RTO 27PS QI; one-minute tourbillon
Functions:	hours, minutes; perpetual calendar with date, weekday, month, moon phase, leap year; 24-hour indication
Case:	platinum, ø 41 mm; sapphire crystal; transparent case back
Price (2010):	on request

PERPETUAL CALENDAR

Reference:	5140J
Movement:	automatic, Patek Philippe Caliber 240 Q
Functions:	hours, minutes; perpetual calendar with date, weekday, month, moon phase, leap year; 24-hour indication
Case:	yellow gold, ø 37.2 mm; sapphire crystal; transparent case back; water-resistant to 3 bar (30 m)
Remarks:	exchangeable platinum case back
Price (2010):	$61,230 (€ 47.450,–)

PERPETUAL CALENDAR

Reference:	5140G
Movement:	automatic, Patek Philippe Caliber 240 Q
Functions:	hours, minutes; perpetual calendar with date, weekday, month, moon phase, leap year; 24-hour indication
Case:	white gold, ø 37.2 mm; sapphire crystal; transparent case back; water-resistant to 3 bar (30 m)
Remarks:	exchangeable platinum case back
Price (2010):	$62,890 (€ 48.730,–)

PERPETUAL CALENDAR

Reference:	5140P
Movement:	automatic, Patek Philippe Caliber 240 Q
Functions:	hours, minutes; perpetual calendar with date, weekday, month, moon phase, leap year; 24-hour indication
Case:	platinum, ø 37.2 mm; sapphire crystal; transparent case back; water-resistant to 3 bar (30 m)
Remarks:	exchangeable platinum case back
Price (2010):	$79,190 (€ 61.360,–)

PERPETUAL CALENDAR

Reference: 5139G
Movement: automatic, Patek Philippe Caliber 240 Q
Functions: hours, minutes; perpetual calendar with date, weekday, month, moon phase, leap year; 24-hour indication
Case: white gold, ø 38 mm; bezel with clous de Paris decoration; sapphire crystal; transparent case back; water-resistant to 3 bar (30 m)
Price (2010): $62,890 (€ 48.730,–)

PERPETUAL CALENDAR

Reference:	5159G
Movement:	automatic, Patek Philippe Caliber 315 QR
Functions:	hours, minutes, sweep seconds; perpetual calendar with date, weekday, month, moon phase, leap year; power reserve display
Case:	white gold, ø 38 mm; sapphire crystal; hunter-style case back with window
Price (2010):	$70,000 (€ 54.230,–)

PERPETUAL CALENDAR

Reference:	5159R
Movement:	automatic, Patek Philippe Caliber 315 QR
Functions:	hours, minutes, sweep seconds; perpetual calendar with date, weekday, month, moon phase, leap year; power reserve display
Case:	rose gold, ø 38 mm; sapphire crystal; hunter-style case back with window
Price (2010):	$70,000 (€ 54.230,–)

CHRONOGRAPH WITH PERPETUAL CALENDAR

Reference:	5970P
Movement:	manual winding, Patek Philippe Caliber CH 27-70 Q (base Nouvelle Lémania)
Functions:	hours, minutes, subsidiary seconds; chronograph; perpetual calendar with date, weekday, month, moon phase, leap year; 24-hour display
Case:	platinum, ø 40 mm; sapphire crystal; transparent case back; water-resistant to 3 bar (30 m)
Price (2010):	$128,910 (€ 99.890,–)

CHRONOGRAPH WITH PERPETUAL CALENDAR

Reference:	5970R
Movement:	manual winding, Patek Philippe Caliber CH 27-70 Q (base Nouvelle Lémania)
Functions:	hours, minutes, subsidiary seconds; chronograph; perpetual calendar with date, weekday, month, moon phase, leap year; 24-hour display
Case:	rose gold, ø 40 mm; sapphire crystal; transparent case back; water-resistant to 3 bar (30 m)
Price (2010):	on request

PERPETUAL CALENDAR

Reference:	5074P
Movement:	automatic, Patek Philippe Caliber R 27 Q
Functions:	hours, minutes; perpetual calendar with date, weekday, month, moon phase, leap year; 24-hour display; minute repeater
Case:	platinum, ø 42 mm; sapphire crystal; transparent case back
Price (2010):	$534,060 (€ 413.840,–)

MINUTE REPEATER

Reference:	5078P
Movement:	automatic, Patek Philippe Caliber R 27 PS
Functions:	hours, minutes, subsidiary seconds; minute repeater
Case:	platinum, ø 38 mm; sapphire crystal; transparent case back
Price (2010):	$331,490 (€ 256.870,–)

MINUTE REPEATER WITH TOURBILLON

Reference:	3939H/P
Movement:	manual winding, Patek Philippe Caliber R TO 27 PS; one-minute tourbillon
Functions:	hours, minutes, subsidiary seconds; minute repeater
Case:	platinum, ø 33.3 mm; sapphire crystal; transparent case back
Price (2010):	on request

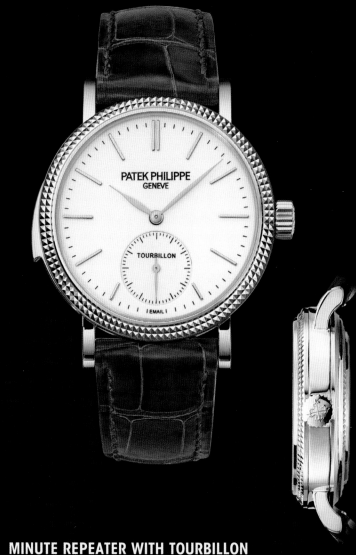

MINUTE REPEATER WITH TOURBILLON

Reference:	3939H/R
Movement:	manual winding, Patek Philippe Caliber R TO 27 PS; one-minute tourbillon
Functions:	hours, minutes, subsidiary seconds; minute repeater
Case:	rose gold, ø 33.3 mm; sapphire crystal; transparent case back
Price (2010):	on request

TECHNICAL DATA

10 JOURS TOURBILLON

Reference:	5101R
Movement:	manual winding, Patek Philippe Caliber TO 28-20 REC 10J PS IRM; one-minute tourbillon; power reserve 240 hours (10 days)
Functions:	hours, minutes, subsidiary seconds; power reserve display
Case:	rose gold, 29.6 x 51.7 mm; sapphire crystal; transparent case back; water-resistant to 3 bar (30 m)
Price (2010):	$280,840 (€ 217.620,–)

10 JOURS TOURBILLON

Reference:	5101P
Movement:	manual winding, Patek Philippe Caliber TO 28-20 REC 10J PS IRM; one-minute tourbillon; power reserve 240 hours (10 days)
Functions:	hours, minutes, subsidiary seconds; power reserve display
Case:	platinum, 29.6 x 51.7 mm; sapphire crystal; transparent case back; water-resistant to 3 bar (30 m)
Price (2010):	$303,860 (€ 235.460,–)

TOURBILLON

Reference:	5339R
Movement:	manual winding, Patek Philippe Caliber R TO 27 PS; one-minute tourbillon
Functions:	hours, minutes, subsidiary seconds; minute repeater
Case:	rose gold, ø 36.4 mm; sapphire crystal; transparent case back
Price (2010):	$451,180 (€ 349.620,–)

SPLIT-SECONDS CHRONOGRAPH

Reference:	5950A
Movement:	manual winding, Patek Philippe Caliber CHR 27-525 PS
Functions:	hours, minutes, subsidiary seconds; split-seconds chronograph
Case:	stainless steel, 44.6 x 37 mm; sapphire crystal; transparent case back; water-resistant to 3 bar (30 m)
Price (2010):	$405,150 (€ 313.950,–)

SPLIT-SECONDS CHRONOGRAPH

Reference:	5959P
Movement:	manual winding, Patek Philippe Caliber CHR 27-525 PS
Functions:	hours, minutes, subsidiary seconds; split-seconds chronograph
Case:	platinum, ø 33.2 mm; sapphire crystal; transparent case back
Price (2010):	$405.150 (€ 313.950,–)

SPLIT-SECONDS CHRONOGRAPH WITH PERPETUAL CALENDAR

Reference:	5004P
Movement:	manual winding, Patek Philippe Caliber CH 27-70 Q (base Nouvelle Lémania)
Functions:	hours, minutes, subsidiary seconds; split-seconds chronograph; perpetual calendar with date, weekday, month, moon phase, leap year; 24-hour display
Case:	platinum, ø 36.7 mm; sapphire crystal; transparent case back; water-resistant to 3 bar (30 m)
Price (2010):	on request

TECHNICAL DATA

CELESTIAL

Reference:	5102 PR
Movement:	automatic, Patek Philippe Caliber 240 LU CL
Functions:	hours, minutes; moon phase and age; map of starry sky
Case:	platinum/rose gold, ø 43.1 mm; sapphire crystal; transparent case back; water-resistant to 3 bar (30 m)
Price (2010):	$221,000 (€ 171.240,–)

SKY MOON

Reference:	5102
Movement:	automatic, Patek Philippe Caliber 240 LU CL
Functions:	hours, minutes; moon phase and age; map of starry sky
Case:	yellow gold, ø 43.1 mm; sapphire crystal; transparent case back; water-resistant to 3 bar (30 m)
Price (2010):	$202,570 (€ 156.970,–)

CELESTIAL

Reference:	6104G
Movement:	automatic, Patek Philippe Caliber 240 LU CLC
Functions:	hours, minutes; date; moon phase and age; map of starry sky
Case:	white gold, ø 44 mm; bezel set with 38 baguette-cut diamonds; sapphire crystal; transparent case back
Price (2010):	$294,650 (€ 228.320,–)

PATEK PHILIPPE
CALATRAVA

Since 1932, the Calatrava has held a place of honor within Patek Philippe's collection. It has become not only a symbol of the brand, but also the epitome of the classic round men's watch. Reduced to the minimum in terms of functions, it unites simplicity, clarity, and elegance in such a timeless way as to have never gone out of style. Today, the Calatrava can be found, for both men and women, in many dial variations, as a time zone model, and even opulently set with gemstones.

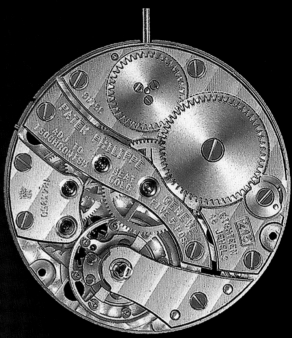

CALATRAVA

Reference:	5196R
Movement:	manual winding, Patek Philippe Caliber 215 PS
Functions:	hours, minutes, subsidiary seconds
Case:	rose gold, ø 37 mm; sapphire crystal
Price (2010):	$16,620 (€ 12.910,–)

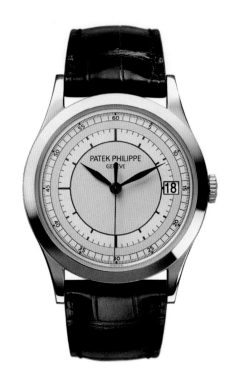

CALATRAVA

Reference:	5127
Movement:	automatic, Patek Philippe Caliber 315 SC
Functions:	hours, minutes, sweep seconds; date
Case:	yellow gold, ø 37 mm; sapphire crystal; transparent case back; screw-in crown
Price (2009):	$18,550 (€ 14.410,–)

CALATRAVA

Reference:	5296G
Movement:	automatic, Patek Philippe Caliber 324 SC
Functions:	hours, minutes, sweep seconds; date
Case:	white gold, ø 38 mm; sapphire crystal; transparent case back
Price (2009):	$19,930 (€ 15.480,–)

CALATRAVA

Reference: 5296R
Movement: automatic, Patek Philippe Caliber 324 SC
Functions: hours, minutes, sweep seconds; date
Case: rose gold, ø 38 mm; sapphire crystal; transparent case back
Price (2009): $19,930 (€ 15.480,–)

TECHNICAL DATA

CALATRAVA

Reference: 5116G
Movement: manual winding, Patek Philippe Caliber 215 PS
Functions: hours, minutes, subsidiary seconds
Case: white gold, ø 36 mm;
bezel decorated with clous de Paris-style guilloché;
sapphire crystal; transparent case back;
water-resistant to 3 bar (30 m)
Remarks: enamel dial
Price (2010): $18,370 (€ 14.270,–)

CALATRAVA

Reference: 5119R
Movement: manual winding, Patek Philippe Caliber 215 PS
Functions: hours, minutes, subsidiary seconds
Case: rose gold, ø 36 mm;
bezel decorated with clous de Paris guilloché;
sapphire crystal;
transparent case back; water-resistant to 3 bar (30 m)
Price (2010): $14,600 (€ 11.340,–)

CALATRAVA

Reference: 5120G
Movement: automatic, Patek Philippe Caliber 240
Functions: hours, minutes
Case: white gold, ø 35 mm;
bezel decorated with clous de Paris guilloché;
sapphire crystal; water-resistant to 3bar (30 m)
Price (2010): € 14.840,–

CALATRAVA TRAVEL TIME

Reference:	5134J
Movement:	manual winding, Patek Philippe Caliber 215 PS FUS 24h
Functions:	hours, minutes, subsidiary seconds; second time zone; 24-hour display
Case:	yellow gold, ø 37 mm; sapphire crystal; transparent case back
Price (2009):	$22,960 (€ 17.840,–)

CALATRAVA

Reference:	6000
Movement:	automatic, Patek Philippe Caliber 240 PS; micro rotor; Seal of Geneva
Functions:	hours, minutes, subsidiary seconds; date
Case:	white gold, ø 37 mm; sapphire crystal; transparent case back
Price (2008):	$19,430 (€ 15.100,–)

CALATRAVA

Reference:	5153J
Movement:	automatic, Patek Philippe Caliber 324 SC
Functions:	hours, minutes, sweep seconds; date
Case:	yellow gold, ø 38 mm; sapphire crystal; transparent hunter case back; water-resistant to 3 bar (30 m)
Remarks:	classic "turban"-style crown
Price (2010):	$23,880 (€ 18.550,–)

TECHNICAL DATA

CALATRAVA

Reference:	4896
Movement:	manual winding, Patek Philippe Caliber 16-250
Functions:	hours, minutes
Case:	white gold, ø 33 mm; bezel set with 72 diamonds; sapphire crystal
Price (2009):	$20,210 (€ 15.700,–)

CALATRAVA

Reference:	4897R
Movement:	manual winding, Patek Philippe Caliber 215 PS
Functions:	hours, minutes
Case:	rose gold, ø 33 mm; bezel set with 72 diamonds; sapphire crystal; transparent case back
Price (2010):	$21,120 (€ 16.410,–)

CALATRAVA TRAVEL TIME

Reference:	4934
Movement:	manual winding, Patek Philippe Caliber 215 PS FUS 24h
Functions:	hours, minutes, subsidiary seconds; second time zone; 24-hour display
Case:	rose gold, ø 35 mm; bezel set with 48 brilliant-cut diamonds; sapphire crystal; transparent case back
Remarks:	mother-of-pearl dial
Price (2009):	$28,470 (€ 22.120,–)

CALATRAVA

Reference:	7119J
Movement:	manual winding, Patek Philippe Caliber 215 PS
Functions:	hours, minutes, subsidiary seconds
Case:	yellow gold, ø 31 mm; bezel decorated with clous de Paris guilloché; sapphire crystal; transparent case back
Price (2010):	$14,240 (€ 11.060,–)

CALATRAVA

Reference:	7120G
Movement:	manual winding, Patek Philippe Caliber 215 PS
Functions:	hours, minutes, subsidiary seconds
Case:	white gold, ø 31 mm; bezel set with 54 diamonds; sapphire crystal; transparent case back
Price (2010):	$22,960 (€ 17.840,–)

PATEK PHILIPPE
NAUTILUS

In the mid-1970s, the time had come: noble manufacture Patek Philippe—until that point known for its highly complicated timepieces—introduced its first sports watch, the Nautilus. High-quality technology coupled with robustness, sportiness, and elegance was the essence of the Nautilus in 1976, and what made it incredibly successful. To this very day—almost three and a half decades later—the design of the original has hardly been modified, proof that Patek Philippe was able to create a style icon that paid absolutely no mind to the capriciousness of trends and times.

NAUTILUS

Reference:	5711/1A
Movement:	automatic, Patek Philippe Caliber 324 SC
Functions:	hours, minutes, sweep seconds; date
Case:	stainless steel, ø 40 mm; sapphire crystal; transparent case back; screw-in crown; water-resistant to 12 bar (120 m)
Price (2010):	$19,280 (€ 14.980,–)

TECHNICAL DATA

NAUTILUS

Reference:	5711R
Movement:	automatic, Patek Philippe Caliber 324 SC
Functions:	hours, minutes, sweep seconds; date
Case:	rose gold, ø 40 mm; sapphire crystal; transparent case back; screw-in crown; water-resistant to 12 bar (120 m)
Price (2010):	on request

NAUTILUS CHRONOGRAPH

Reference:	5980/1A
Movement:	automatic, Patek Philippe Caliber CH-28-520 C; column-wheel control of chronograph
Functions:	hours, minutes, sweep seconds; chronograph; date
Case:	stainless steel, ø 40.5 mm; sapphire crystal; transparent case back; screw-in crown; water-resistant to 12 bar (120 m)
Price (2009):	$37,010 (€ 28.750,–)

NAUTILUS CHRONOGRAPH

Reference:	5980R
Movement:	automatic, Patek Philippe Caliber CH-28-520 C; column-wheel control of chronograph
Functions:	hours, minutes, sweep seconds; chronograph; date
Case:	rose gold, ø 40.5 mm; sapphire crystal; transparent case back; screw-in crown; water-resistant to 12 bar (120 m)
Price (2010):	$45,000 (€ 34.960,–)

TECHNICAL DATA

NAUTILUS POWER RESERVE

Reference:	5712/1A
Movement:	automatic, Patek Philippe Caliber 240 PS; micro rotor; Seal of Geneva
Functions:	hours, minutes, subsidiary seconds; date; moon phase; power reserve display
Case:	stainless steel, ø 43 mm; sapphire crystal; transparent case back; screw-in crown; water-resistant to 6 bar (60 m)
Price (2008):	$23,040 (€ 17.900,–)

NAUTILUS ANNUAL CALENDAR

Reference: 5726A

Movement: automatic, Patek Philippe Caliber 324 S QA LU 24h

Functions: hours, minutes, sweep seconds; annual calendar with date, weekday, month, moon phase; 24-hour display

Case: stainless steel, ø 40.5 mm; sapphire crystal; transparent case back; screw-in crown; water-resistant to 12 bar (120 m)

Price (2010): $31,230 (€ 24.260,–)

TECHNICAL DATA

NAUTILUS

Reference:	7010/1R
Movement:	quartz, Patek Philippe Caliber E 23 SC
Functions:	hours, minutes, sweep seconds; date
Case:	rose gold, ø 32 mm; bezel set with 46 diamonds; sapphire crystal; water-resistant to 6 bar (60 m)
Price (2010):	$31,230 (€ 24.260,–)

NAUTILUS

Reference:	7010G
Movement:	quartz, Patek Philippe Caliber E 23 SC
Functions:	hours, minutes, sweep seconds; date
Case:	white gold, ø 32 mm; bezel set with 46 diamonds; sapphire crystal; water-resistant to 6 bar (60 m)
Price (2010):	$22,960 (€ 17.840,–)

NAUTILUS

Reference:	2021/1G
Movement:	automatic, Patek Philippe Caliber 324 SC
Functions:	hours, minutes, sweep seconds; date
Case:	white gold, ø 37 mm; case, dial and strap set with a total of 2,328 diamonds; sapphire crystal; transparent case back; water-resistant to 3 bar (30 m)
Price (2010):	on request

PATEK PHILIPPE
AQUANAUT

In 1997, the Aquanaut was introduced as the "little brother" to the sports watch line Nautilus, a model that had already proven successful for more than three decades. The Aquanaut was aimed at a younger clientele looking for an elegant sports watch of manufacture quality, for everyday wear. The Aquanaut has always been available in a stainless steel case, which represents something of a rarity in the manufacture's gold-dominated collection. There continue to be two sizes to choose from: the "large" at 38 mm in diameter and the "extra-large," which comes in at 40 mm. The diameter of the ladies' Luce is more proportionate to the feminine wrist, with its 35 mm case.

AQUANAUT

Reference:	5167A
Movement:	automatic, Patek Philippe Caliber 324 SC; Seal of Geneva
Functions:	hours, minutes, sweep seconds; date
Case:	stainless steel; ø 40 mm; sapphire crystal; transparent case back; screw-in crown; water-resistant to 12 bar (120 m)
Price (2009):	$14,700 (€ 11.420,–)

AQUANAUT

Reference:	5167A
Movement:	automatic, Patek Philippe Caliber 324 SC; Seal of Geneva
Functions:	hours, minutes, sweep seconds; date
Case:	stainless steel, ø 40 mm; sapphire crystal; transparent case back; screw-in crown; water-resistant to 12 bar (120 m)
Price (2009):	$16,990 (€ 13.200,–)

AQUANAUT

Reference:	5167/1A
Movement:	automatic, Patek Philippe Caliber 324 SC; Seal of Geneva
Functions:	hours, minutes, sweep seconds; date
Case:	stainless steel, ø 38 mm; sapphire crystal; transparent case back; screw-in crown; water-resistant to 12 bar (120 m)
Price (2009):	$14,700 (€ 11.420,–)

AQUANAUT

Reference:	5167A
Movement:	automatic, Patek Philippe Caliber 324 SC; Seal of Geneva
Functions:	hours, minutes, sweep seconds; date
Case:	rose gold, ø 40 mm; sapphire crystal; transparent case back; screw-in crown; water-resistant to 12 bar (120m)
Price (2009):	$26,180 (€ 20.340,–)

AQUANAUT LUCE

Reference:	5067
Movement:	quartz, Patek Philippe Caliber E 23 SC
Functions:	hours, minutes, sweep seconds; date
Case:	stainless steel, ø 35.2 mm; bezel set with 46 diamonds; sapphire crystal; transparent case back; screw-in crown; water-resistant to 6 bar (60 m)
Price (2007):	$10,940 (€ 8500,–)

AQUANAUT LUCE

Reference:	5067
Movement:	quartz, Patek Philippe Caliber E 23 SC
Functions:	hours, minutes, sweep seconds; date
Case:	stainless steel, ø 35.2 mm; bezel set with 46 diamonds; sapphire crystal; transparent case back; screw-in crown; water-resistant to 6 bar (60 m)
Price (2007):	$12,590 (€ 9780,–)

AQUANAUT LUCE

Reference:	5068R
Movement:	manual winding, Patek Philippe Caliber 324 SC
Functions:	hours, minutes, sweep seconds; date
Case:	stainless steel, ø 35.2 mm; bezel set with 46 diamonds; sapphire crystal; transparent case back; screw-in crown; water-resistant to 12 bar (120 m)
Price (2010):	$29,390 (€ 22.830,–)

PATEK PHILIPPE
ELLIPSE D'OR

Since its market launch in 1968, the Ellipse d'Or has become one of the grand classics of the Patek Philippe collection. This is most likely so because of its unmistakable case, whose rounded square shape is ideally proportioned. Thus, the Ellipse d'Or has hardly changed over the course of the last forty years. One of the few changes is a barely noticeable increase in size, made in order to fit the modern idea of taste. Another comprises a move to ultra-flat automatic Caliber 240 (2.53 mm in height), which replaces the previous hand-wound movement originally used.

ELLIPSE D'OR (1968)

Reference:	3548/1
Movement:	manual winding, Patek Philippe Caliber 23-300PM; rhodium-plated, Seal of Geneva
Functions:	hours, minutes
Case:	yellow gold, 32 x 27 mm; push-down case back
Price (2009):	$1,930 (€ 1500,–)

ELLIPSE D'OR

Reference:	3738/100 J
Movement:	automatic, Patek Philippe Caliber 240
Functions:	hours, minutes
Case:	yellow gold, 35.6 x 31.1 mm; sapphire crystal
Price (2009):	$18,190 (€ 14.130,–)

TECHNICAL DATA

ELLIPSE D'OR

Reference:	3738/100 J
Movement:	automatic, Patek Philippe Caliber 240
Functions:	hours, minutes
Case:	rose gold, 35.6 x 31.1 mm; sapphire crystal
Price (2009):	$19,570 (€ 15.200,–)

ELLIPSE D'OR

Reference:	3738/100 J
Movement:	automatic, Patek Philippe Caliber 240
Functions:	hours, minutes
Case:	white gold, 35.6 x 31.1 mm; sapphire crystal
Price (2009):	$19,570 (€ 15.200,–)

ELLIPSE D'OR

Reference: 5738P
Movement: automatic, Patek Philippe Caliber 240
Functions: hours, minutes
Case: platinum, 39.5 x 34.5 mm; sapphire crystal
Price (2010): $37,650 (€ 29.250,–)

PATEK PHILIPPE
GONDOLO

The Gondolo model family has been enriching the Patek Philippe collection since 1993. These filigreed watches, inspired by classics from the 1930s, transport the elegance and design language of Art Deco, with its strict geometry and clean lines, into the twenty-first century. Along with two- and three-hand men's models, this model family also boasts an annual calendar, which unites Patek Philippe's scrupulous horological demands with the sleek design of the unmistakable Gondolo.

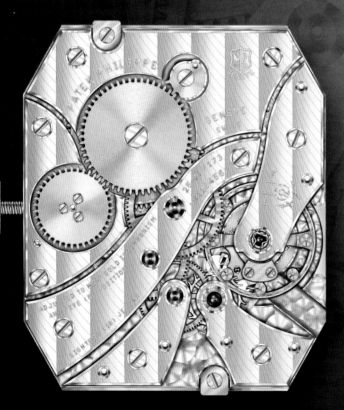

GONDOLO

Reference:	5124J
Movement:	manual winding, Patek Philippe Caliber 25-21 REC PS
Functions:	hours, minutes, subsidiary seconds; date
Case:	yellow gold, 33.4 x 43 mm; sapphire crystal; transparent case back
Price (2009):	$17,450 (€ 13.560,–)

GONDOLO

Reference:	5124G
Movement:	manual winding, Patek Philippe Caliber 25-21 REC PS
Functions:	hours, minutes, subsidiary seconds
Case:	white gold, 33 x 43 mm; sapphire crystal; transparent case back
Price (2009):	$18,830 (€ 14.630,–)

CHRONOMETRO GONDOLO

Reference:	5098R
Movement:	manual winding, Patek Philippe Caliber 25-21 REC
Functions:	hours, minutes
Case:	rose gold, 32 x 42 mm; sapphire crystal; transparent case back; water-resistant to 3 bar (30 m)
Price (2009):	$20,690 (€ 20.690,–)

CHRONOMETRO GONDOLO

Reference:	5098P
Movement:	manual winding, Patek Philippe Caliber 25-21 REC
Functions:	hours, minutes
Case:	platinum, 32 x 42 mm; sapphire crystal; transparent case back; water-resistant to 3 bar (30 m)
Price (2009):	$36,740 (€ 28.540,–)

GONDOLO CALENDARIO

Reference: 5135G

Movement: automatic, Patek Philippe Caliber 324 S QA LU 24 H

Functions: hours, minutes, sweep seconds; annual calendar with date, weekday, month, moon phase; 24-hour display

Case: white gold, 38 x 51 mm, sapphire crystal; transparent case back

Price (2009): $35,360 (€ 27.470,–)

TECHNICAL DATA

GONDOLO

Reference:	5111G
Movement:	manual winding, Patek Philippe Caliber 215 PS
Functions:	hours, minutes, subsidiary seconds
Case:	white gold, 47.8 x 32.9 mm; sapphire crystal; transparent case back
Price (2006):	$17,250 (€ 13.400,–)

GONDOLO TRAPÈZE

Reference:	5489R
Movement:	manual winding, Patek Philippe Caliber 215; Seal of Geneva
Functions:	hours, minutes
Case:	rose gold, 32.5 x 34 mm; sapphire crystal
Price (2006):	$17,000 (€ 13.200,–)

GONDOLO GEMMA

Reference:	4991R
Movement:	manual winding, Patek Philippe Caliber 16-250; Seal of Geneva
Functions:	hours, minutes
Case:	rose gold, 37.2 x 22.4 mm; bezel and strap lugs set with 72 diamonds; sapphire crystal; transparent case back
Remarks:	mother-of-pearl dial
Price (2008):	$22,330 (€ 17.350,–)

GONDOLO GEMMA

Reference:	4980G
Movement:	quartz, Patek Philippe Caliber E 15
Functions:	hours, minutes
Case:	white gold, 37.2 x 22.4 mm; sapphire crystal
Price (2008):	$15,150 (€ 11.770,–)

PATEK PHILIPPE®